Rodrigo Felipe da Silva Mendes
Flávia Gonçalves Fernandes

Programming with LEGO® SPIKE(TM) Prime and Python for High School

Rodrigo Felipe da Silva Mendes
Flávia Gonçalves Fernandes

Programming with LEGO® SPIKE(TM) Prime and Python for High School

Developing Computing Skills in 1st Year Students

ScienciaScripts

Imprint
Any brand names and product names mentioned in this book are subject to trademark, brand or patent protection and are trademarks or registered trademarks of their respective holders. The use of brand names, product names, common names, trade names, product descriptions etc. even without a particular marking in this work is in no way to be construed to mean that such names may be regarded as unrestricted in respect of trademark and brand protection legislation and could thus be used by anyone.

Cover image: www.ingimage.com

This book is a translation from the original published under ISBN 978-620-6-76233-1.

Publisher:
Sciencia Scripts
is a trademark of
Dodo Books Indian Ocean Ltd. and OmniScriptum S.R.L publishing group

120 High Road, East Finchley, London, N2 9ED, United Kingdom
Str. Armeneasca 28/1, office 1, Chisinau MD-2012, Republic of Moldova, Europe
Managing Directors: Ieva Konstantinova, Victoria Ursu
info@omniscriptum.com

Printed at: see last page
ISBN: 978-620-8-52286-5

THANKS

First and foremost, I thank God for the gift of life and the wisdom he has given me. I thank my advisor Flávia for all her help and patience during the specialization and in the complicated moments that life throws at us. Thank you to my family, especially my wife, Priscilla, who supported me and gave me strength at all times. I thank my children, Ana Beatriz, my beautiful and precious little one, and Samuel, the newest member of the family, my beloved children. Thank you to the friends that life has given me and to my fellow students who, during this year, have grown with me in a unique way. I couldn't fail to thank my parents, Washington and Adriana, who have always given me love, strength and support. Thank you to the other teachers on the course, who have always made themselves available to help me. I would like to thank the school taking part in this project, its coordinators and management, who made the classes available for the project to be carried out; this help was invaluable in obtaining this degree. To the other colleagues and friends I haven't mentioned, please know that you have contributed in a unique way to this stage of my life. Thank you all very much!

SUMMARY

This text highlights the growing importance of teaching programming in basic education, evidenced both by international initiatives and by academic research that analyzes effective teaching methods. In the UK, making programming compulsory in the school curriculum demonstrates an effort to align education with contemporary technical demands. Digital literacy is highlighted as fundamental to preparing young people for a job market that demands programming skills. The use of tools such as platforms and programming languages to integrate computational thinking and digital literacy are excellent pedagogical tools and extremely effective in basic education. These efforts highlight the need to develop programming skills in students, preparing them for future challenges. In line with the BNCC guidelines, the use of resources such as *Python* and the *LEGO KIT® SPIKE™ PRIME* has proved to be effective in making learning more interactive and motivating for students in the first year of the new high school, as evidenced by the experiments applied in this work.

Keywords: Computational thinking. Digital Literacy . *Python*.

ABSTRACT

This text highlights the growing importance of teaching programming in basic education, as evidenced by both international initiatives and academic research that analyze effective teaching methods. In the United Kingdom, the requirement of programming in the school curriculum demonstrates an effort to align education with contemporary technical demands. Digital literacy is emphasized as essential for preparing young people for a job market that requires programming skills. The use of tools such as platforms and programming languages to integrate computational thinking and digital literacy are excellent pedagogical tools and extremely effective in basic education. These efforts underscore the need to develop programming skills in students, preparing them for future challenges. Aligned with the guidelines of the BNCC (Brazilian National Common Core Curriculum), the use of resources like Python and the LEGO® SPIKE™ PRIME KIT has proven effective in making learning more interactive and motivating for 1st-year high school students, as evidenced by the experiences applied in this work.

Keywords: Computational Thinking. Digital Literacy. Python.

SUMMARY

1 INTRODUCTION

As the world becomes increasingly digital, education in technology takes on a central role in the training of future professionals capable of facing modern challenges. In Brazil, the National Common Core Curriculum (BRASIL, 2018, p. 531) highlights the importance of integrating technological and computational skills from basic education and establishes that "[...] using the basic concepts of a programming language in the implementation of algorithms written in ordinary and/or mathematical language" (BRASIL, 2018, p. 531).

One of the ways to achieve this integration is by teaching programming and robotics, subjects that foster not only technical knowledge, but also problem-solving skills, logic and creativity.

This work proposes the implementation of a teaching methodology that uses the Python programming language in conjunction with the *LEGO® SPIKE™ PRIME KIT* , aimed at 1st year high school students. The *LEGO® SPIKE™ PRIME KIT*, an innovative educational tool, offers a robust platform for exploring basic robotics and programming concepts in a practical and engaging way. The choice of Python, due to its clear syntax and wide applicability, aims to facilitate students' first contact with programming, providing a smooth and motivating learning curve.

Integrating the teaching of Python and robotics with the *LEGO® SPIKE™ PRIME KIT* into the curriculum of the first year of secondary school, in accordance with the guidelines of the National Common Curriculum Base (BRASIL, 2018, p. 511), can not only increase students' interest in STEM areas (Science, Technology, Engineering and Mathematics), but also better prepare them for future academic and professional challenges.

In general, the main objective of this work was to investigate and propose techniques for introducing programming notions with Python using the *LEGO KIT® SPIKE™ PRIME* to students in the 1st year of the new high school, in order to motivate more students to seek out programming-related courses and to try to improve the way programming is introduced Marques et al. (2011).

This paper reports on the experience gained in developing some of the techniques used in an introductory workshop on programming with Python for students in the 1st year of the new high school in a school located in the state of Rio de Janeiro, as a way of encouraging the replication of the acceptance results found by the students and the possible application in other classes and schools.

This paper is organized as follows. Section 2 presents the Objectives. Section 3 presents the justification. Section 4 presents the Theoretical Review. Section 5 presents the Methodology adopted to carry out this work. Section 6 presents the analysis of the results. Section 7 presents the conclusions. Finally, Section 8 presents the references.

2 OBJECTIVES

2.1 GENERAL OBJECTIVE

Develop programming and computational thinking skills in 1st year high school students, using the *LEGO KIT® SPIKE™ PRIME* and the *Python* language, in accordance with the BNCC guidelines.

2.1.1 Specific objectives

- Introduce basic concepts of programming and robotics.
- Stimulate logical and creative thinking and problem solving.
- Promote digital culture and teamwork skills.
- Apply theoretical knowledge in practical contexts and interactive projects.

3 JUSTICE

The implementation of this didactic sequence, focused on programming with *LEGO® SPIKE™ PRIME* and *Python* for 1st year high school students, aligned with the Common National Curriculum Base (BRASIL, 2018, p. 531), emerges from a conjunction of educational, technological and social factors that highlight the importance of integrating computational and critical thinking skills into the school curriculum (VIEIRA et al., 2022). This proposal seeks to meet various essential educational needs and objectives.

We live in a digital age, in which technology permeates all areas of human life. It is essential that education prepares students with the skills needed to navigate this technological world, including digital competencies, critical thinking, problem-solving and teamwork. The Common National Curriculum Base emphasizes the importance of developing skills that transcend factual knowledge, such as scientific thinking, digital culture and collaborative work (BRASIL, 2018, p. 528). This project aligns directly with these objectives, offering a practical and integrated approach to achieving them.

Programming is a powerful tool for developing computational thinking, an essential skill that allows students not only to understand the digital world around them, but also to actively participate in building it (BACICH, 2018). Through programming, students learn to break down complex problems, recognize patterns, abstract and develop solutions step by step.

Using the *LEGO® SPIKE™ PRIME KIT* makes learning to program tangible, interactive and fun. By building and programming their own robots, students see the immediate results of their work, which can significantly increase engagement and motivation to learn (SIQUEIRA, 2021). In addition to specific technical programming skills, the project promotes the development of transversal skills such as creativity, collaboration and communication. These are essential skills that will benefit students in whatever career or life path they choose to follow.

With the rapid advancement of technology, many of the careers of the future will require a deep understanding of computing and technology (SILVA NETO et al., 2020). By introducing students to programming and computational thinking from an early age, this project prepares them for these future challenges, opening doors to opportunities in Science, Technology, Engineering and Mathematics (STEM) and beyond (CHAVES, 2023, p. 37).

4 THEORETICAL REVIEW

This research addresses the role of Educational Robotics in student education, as well as the potential of Computer Programming as a methodological tool to mediate studies and the learning process. It also highlights the relevance of programming knowledge for the job market, regardless of the area of activity. In this context, it is clear that the student must be fully involved in the learning process, so that pedagogical practice acquires meaning, arouses interest and promotes the integral development of the student as a citizen.

To achieve these objectives, it is essential that the methodologies used provide creative space for the student, encouraging them to be investigators and to have a voice and action in the learning process. As Campos, Wodewotzki and Jacobini (2018, p. 2) point out, this approach is essential for effective educational training.

This definition covers several of the objectives of this work and, for this reason, it is considered relevant to discuss working with projects. Malheiros (2008) points out that projects are closely related to the interests and objectives of those who develop them, and that objectives and goals point to the results that are desired and strived for. In addition, the author points out that "a project consists of the anticipation of an action that involves reference to the future" (MALHEIROS, 2008, p. 56), but differs from a prospective vision that moves away from reality.

In this sense, the activity needs to be directly linked to the students' current or future reality and must necessarily encourage active student participation. According to Campos, Wodewotzki and Jacobini (2018), this participation is related to the study of situations present in the student's daily life, stimulating various reflections that involve, in addition to curricular aspects, multiple issues related to such situations. With specific regard to the discipline in which this activity takes place, the "application of mathematics to solve real problems also generates the need to collect data and simplify situations in reality" (CAMPOS et al., 2018, p. 49).

Finally, it is essential that projects work with real data; relate data to the context in which they are inserted; require students to interpret the results; allow activities to be carried out in groups to encourage debate between students; and promote judgments about the validity of conclusions (allowing the sharing of conclusions with the class and the presentation of justifications) (CAMPOS et al., 2018) . These aspects are present in the proposal of this work.

The pedagogical proposal described in the following sections is based on the project methodology. As well as looking at this method of enhancing student involvement, the next few subsections also present a reference on the main elements of this work: Educational Robotics and Computer Programming. These initiatives and studies reinforce the theme of our work, which focuses on incorporating the teaching of programming into the curriculum of the first year of secondary school through the use of the Python language and the *LEGO KIT® SPIKE™ PRIME*. This approach not only aligns with the BNCC guidelines for the insertion of digital skills from basic education, but also aims to offer a practical and engaging approach that can motivate students and prepare them for the technological demands of the future.

4.1 DIGITAL TECHNOLOGIES

The importance of computer programming is a central aspect of this course completion work, being the main element of the pedagogical approach adopted. As described by Campos et al. (2018), the influence of information technology is evident, whether as operational support or as a means of tackling recurring challenges in educational environments, such as the lack of student engagement and the absence of skills needed for the job market. Therefore, the relevance of technologies applied to the project method stands out, especially in terms of stimulating student interest and developing essential skills for the current job market, which demands professionals trained in the digital sector.

In the contemporary scenario, Borba, Almeida and Gracias (2019) highlight the rapid evolution of technological innovations that are becoming increasingly integrated into everyday life, with more advanced personal computers and faster internet connections. These authors point out that, in this context, new versions of "programming languages, operating systems, software, internet applications, social networks and multifunctional portable electronic devices such as notebooks, tablets, smartphones, digital cameras, among others" are emerging (Borba et al. 2019, p. 21). However, these resources are still underutilized in the educational context, even transcending the boundaries of the classroom.

It is crucial to recognize this interaction, since technological innovation provides alternative educational environments and, specifically, opportunities for Mathematics Education. Educational institutions are lagging behind in incorporating these technologies into the curriculum, which is contradictory considering that students already interact with these tools on a daily basis. In order to take advantage of these opportunities, it is essential to investigate the use of technological innovations in education, the evolution of mathematical research driven by technology and the types of activities that can be developed in this context. This final paper seeks to contribute to these discussions, emphasizing the importance of a continuous progression in learning programming languages, from basic education to higher education.

In short, digital technologies are redefining our perception of being human, influencing social norms and everyday practices. This transformation occurs at different speeds inside and outside of school, widening the gap between the experiences of teachers and students (Borba et al., 2019). The next section will look at opportunities for teaching computer programming, with a focus on the Block Programming and *Python* languages.

4.2 COMPUTATIONAL THINKING

Computational thinking is an essential skill recommended for everyone, not just scientists, as it contributes significantly to the development of skills such as reading, writing and improving logical thinking (WING, 2006). Applying this skill in the educational context, especially when teaching programming with *Python* and using the *LEGO® SPIKE™ PRIME KIT* for educational robotics, allows students to develop the ability to solve complex problems in a structured and creative way.

The practice of computational thinking involves a series of skills such as problem solving, building systems and understanding human behavior. This occurs through abstraction and decomposition techniques, which allow a larger problem to be broken down into smaller parts, making it easier to solve in an efficient and practical way (WING, 2006). In the context of teaching programming with *Python*, this approach enables students to understand algorithms and logical structures in a more tangible way, especially when integrating learning with robotic projects using the *LEGO® SPIKE™ PRIME KIT*

When students are presented with problems through practical activities, such as programming robots, they can apply decomposition techniques to break the task down into small steps and work on each one in a focused way. This not only facilitates the process of identifying problems, but also allows them to recognize patterns and build efficient solutions. The techniques used in computational thinking - decomposition, pattern recognition, abstraction and algorithms - are applied directly to programming and robotics activities, providing more effective and interactive learning (BRACKMANN, 2017).

In addition to its direct applications in the field of programming, computational thinking is also present in several other disciplines. It plays an important role in scientific research and the humanities, allowing researchers in areas such as geology, biology, psychology and medicine to analyze large data sets and find solutions to complex problems (BUNDY, 2007). By integrating computational thinking into the school curriculum, students not only develop technical skills, but are also prepared to face challenges in various areas of knowledge.

As WING (2008) points out, the essence of computational thinking is abstraction. In programming with *Python* and developing robotic projects with the *LEGO® SPIKE™ PRIME KIT*, students learn to abstract concepts that go beyond the physical dimensions of time and space. This practice encourages the construction of symbolic and complex solutions, making learning deeper and more meaningful. In this way, computational thinking is fundamental not only for teaching programming, but for training individuals who are prepared for a society that is increasingly dependent on technology.

4.3 BLOCK PROGRAMMING

Today, the ability to program is seen as an essential 21st century skill. With this in mind, schools and universities are rapidly adopting new curricula that incorporate computer science and logical reasoning into areas that previously didn't involve programming. The block-based programming method is gaining popularity as a simpler and more efficient way of teaching programming concepts to beginners, using a range of tools such as the Scratch and Alice platforms. In general, programming with blocks offers a more interactive and visual experience compared to conventional programming, where the blocks function as programming commands that can be combined in different ways, resulting in different outputs (WERNTROP; WILENSKY, 2015).

In the first analysis, the researchers explored how students perceive the visual characteristics and interactivity of block programming techniques in contrast to conventional programming methods that do not employ graphic elements. As observed, there was an improvement in student performance on tasks that incorporated visual elements into the programming. However, the authors point to challenges in determining which specific aspects of blocks facilitate understanding compared to traditional textual approaches to programming, given that multiple factors can affect the interpretation of code expressed through blocks (WERNTROP; WILENSKY, 2015).

4.3.1 SCRATCH

Scratch is a visual programming language developed and maintained by the Lifelong Kindergarten group at the Massachusetts Institute of Technology (MIT). Created in 2007, the language was initially designed for an audience aged between 8 and 16, but today it is used by people of all age groups. Scratch uses visual and multimedia elements, allowing sequences to be created using animations. This positive approach to learning programming is achieved through "blocks" that represent specific functionalities, allowing users to drag blocks that symbolize programming commands to create games, animations and interactions (REZENDE; BISPO, 2018).

As described by Mitchel Resnick, Scratch is an open-source programming language that allows you to create interactive games, stories and animations using programming blocks. In addition, projects developed in Scratch can be shared with the community. As the children work on their projects, they learn to think creatively, improve their logical thinking and develop teamwork skills, acquiring important concepts in the area of computing.

In the context of the *LEGO® SPIKE™ PRIME App* platform, which also uses programming blocks, Scratch can be a valuable complementary tool, offering a visual environment where learners can program and create their own interactive narratives and projects. Block programming in both the *LEGO® SPIKE™ PRIME App* and Scratch simplifies the complexity of textual programming language syntax, making it easier to understand fundamental programming logic concepts. The *LEGO® SPIKE™ PRIME App* platform enables students to program physical robots using visual blocks, while Scratch can serve as an alternative for practicing and reinforcing these concepts in a purely digital environment.

When programming with blocks, whether in the *LEGO® SPIKE™ PRIME App* or in Scratch, the user organizes the components following a logical line of reasoning, trying to build a coherent sequence of commands. In the case of the *LEGO® SPIKE™ PRIME App*, block programming is geared towards robotics, allowing students to see the results of their programming instructions in physical robot actions. In Scratch, learners develop purely digital interactive projects, such as animations and games, which also help to reinforce logical thinking and problem solving.

Both platforms encourage the development of important skills, such as logical reasoning, creativity, systems thinking and problem solving, as highlighted by Castro (2017, p. 39):

> Scratch enables users to learn through various skills such as: Logical Reasoning, Creativity, Systemic Thinking, Problem Solving, in a fun way and using technology, it is also possible to work collaboratively by sharing projects on the program's website. Students who use
> Scratch learns to fit blocks together like a puzzle or a lego game in a logical way.

By using these block-based programming tools, students have the opportunity to explore and experience the world of programming in a practical, accessible and intuitive way. This process makes it easier to visualize and manipulate programming logic, making learning more concrete and applicable. Therefore, both Scratch and the *LEGO® SPIKE™ PRIME App* are powerful tools for practicing programming, each offering a distinct environment for developing skills in programming, robotics and computational thinking (RESNICK et al., 2009).

In this way, Scratch establishes itself as an environment where learners have the freedom to develop and program their own interactive stories. The essence of the Scratch language lies in shaping an interactive space that challenges students to engage and overcome obstacles, using the knowledge they already have as a foundation. This process requires the active fostering of creativity, which is essential for solving problems. This promotion of creativity is harmoniously incorporated into programming logic, making it more intuitive and rewarding, as Scratch was designed to simplify the complexities normally found in the syntax of traditional programming languages. As Castro (2017, p. 39) points out:

> Scratch allows users to learn through various skills such as: Logical Reasoning, Creativity, Systemic Thinking, Problem Solving, in a fun way and using technology, it is also possible to work collaboratively by sharing projects on the program's website. Students who use
> Scratch learns to fit blocks together like a puzzle or a lego game in a logical way.

When programming with Scratch (Figure 1), which uses a system of blocks, the user organizes these components following their line of reasoning, with the aim of building a logical sequence within the project. This allows the learner not only to visualize the logical structure of their program, but also to manipulate it in a tangible way, facilitating the understanding of programming principles and the practical application of the knowledge acquired. Scratch is therefore not just a programming tool, but a means of personal expression, where prior knowledge and individual creativity are valued and encouraged in the educational process (RESNICK et al., 2009).

Figure1 - Programming interface with Scratch

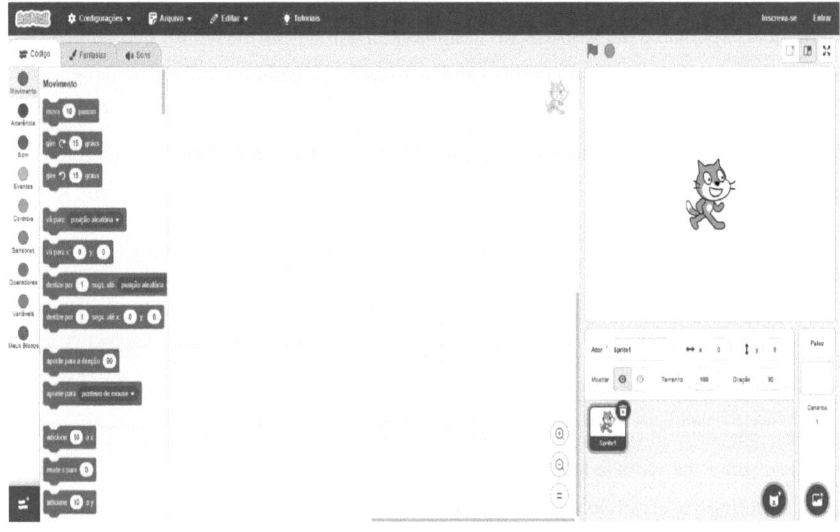

Source: The author (2024)

4.4 EDUCATIONAL ROBOTICS

According to Harel and Papert (1991), technology has the capacity to generate multiple forms of representation, unlike material and analog instruments. Their epistemological model shares the view that instruction is the construction of a knowledge structure, regardless of the contexts in which learning takes place.

According to Machado (2017), schools are part of globalization, which requires development in various areas. Modernization comes about through new ways of thinking and operating, changing everyday life. Technologies are part of the lives of students and educators and are widely used.

In the application of Educational Robotics, the teacher is not the only provider of information and knowledge. The student is challenged to reflect on the problem to be solved, seeking solutions through formulations and applications in various areas, such as Mathematics, Physics and Computing (ALMEIDA, 2007).

D'Abreu et al. (2013) show that Educational Robotics is increasingly effective and attractive in the educational context. It expands the use of digital resources, incorporating concepts of design, progress and programming through electronic devices. Students have the opportunity to improve and share this knowledge, realizing that they are not only users, but also capable of building and controlling robotic programs to solve problems that they themselves identify.

Robotics is considered a multidisciplinary field, covering areas such as electronics, music, physics, mathematics, the arts, computer science, engineering and artificial intelligence. Depending on the perspective, it offers qualities in various branches, making it a significant pedagogical potential (RIBEIRO, 2011).

According to (CAMBRUZZI , 2015) , (SILVA, 2019) and (FIA, 2021), Educational Robotics, as an active learning methodology, aims to train more proactive students who take responsibility for their own learning process. This change in attitude helps children and adolescents to move away from the role of mere spectators and become protagonists in the construction of their knowledge. Depending on the context, robotics can also serve purposes such as:

- Increasing interest in scientific and technological topics;
- Making lessons more dynamic and fun;
- Facilitate the learning of subjects such as Physics, Mathematics, among others;
- Providing more interaction between educators and students;
- Enrich the curriculum with technology-oriented subjects;
- Strengthen critical thinking and problem solving through new tools;
- To bring students of different profiles closer together by putting them in groups to build robots;
- To highlight the connections between different disciplines and their application in everyday life;
- Preparing students for the job market, which is full of unfilled vacancies in the field of technology.

The first research into Educational Robotics in Brazil dates back to 1976, when a group of professors from the State University of Campinas (UNICAMP) began investigating the use of computers in education. This research involved activities related to the LOGO environment.

According to (NUNES, 2020), throughout the educational journey, robotics has been a valuable tool for making learning more accessible and stimulating. Among the areas directly related to robotics, Physics, Electronics, Mechanics and Computer Science stand out. All these disciplines are based on mathematics, considered the mother of all sciences.

For (CARNEIRO, 2023), Educational Robotics offers an excellent way of making mathematical concepts concrete and applicable at different levels of education. In the context of Educational Robotics, it is possible to explore the areas of Geometry and Trigonometry in particular, with clear applications. In addition, Arithmetic and Calculus also play an important role in robotics challenges, from mental calculations to refining estimates. Through these areas, robotics makes it possible to develop activities that promote problem-based learning. Changes in this field are occurring rapidly, pushing education towards new horizons.

In Brazil, educational robots still don't have a specific national public policy. Many questions remain open regarding the use of robotics in education. In different educational contexts, progress is not uniform and is limited to individual cases. In addition, there is no systematic strategy for adopting this new tool and incorporating it into the teaching curriculum at different levels of education (CAMPOS, 2017).

Despite the many difficulties faced by Brazilian education, it is easy to find studies and articles focusing on the use of robots as a teaching resource. These materials can help educators better understand the educational applications of these technologies (MORAES, 2010).

For (CAMPOS, 2017). Educational Robotics has undergone remarkable development processes in Brazil. However, in order for it to reach its full potential, broader and more comprehensive investment is needed across the board. This investment will not only boost the field of robotics, but will also make learning more enriching and accessible to students, encouraging a new way of thinking and learning.

4.5 ROBOTICS WITH LEGO

The *LEGO* Robotics platform® *Mindstorms®* was built on Logo, "a programming language and pedagogical approach developed by Dr. Seymour Papert during the 1960s at the Artificial Intelligence Laboratory" (PIRES; SILVA, 2012, p. 3). In 1960, in his Artificial Intelligence Laboratory, Dr. Seymour Papert innovated by integrating programming language with educational philosophy. The pedagogical basis of the project was inspired by Papert's work and learning theories.

LEGO® , in collaboration with companies such as the Brazilian publisher Edacom, advanced the development of the Zoom® project and program, intended for use in the educational context (LIMA, 2017). In 1986, the synergy between MIT[1] and LEGO® resulted in the creation of the first *software* called *LEGO® Technic Computer Control*, designed to manage robots equipped with motors and sensors (LIMA, 2017, p. 22). This technological innovation progressed until the launch of *LEGO® Mindstorms® Education RCX (Robotic Command Explorer)* in 1998. Later, in 2006, LEGO® *Mindstorms® Education NXT (Next)* was introduced, followed by *LEGO® Mindstorms® Education EV3* (Evolution) in 2013, *LEGO® SPIKE™ PRIME /LEGO® ROBÔ INVENTOR MINDSTORMS®* , which is the basis of this study.

4.6 THE LEGO EDUCATION SPIKE PRIME KIT

The *LEGO® Education SPIKE™ Prime* platform is the successor to the *LEGO® Mindstorms®* range, offering an innovative and engaging experience for students taking their first steps into the world of robotics. This *kit* (figure 2) is designed to be intuitive and stimulating, with around 528 pieces that are easy to assemble and disassemble, promoting practical and creative learning.

[1] MIT - *Massachusetts Institute of Technology*

Figure2 - LEGO® Education SPIKE™ Prime kit

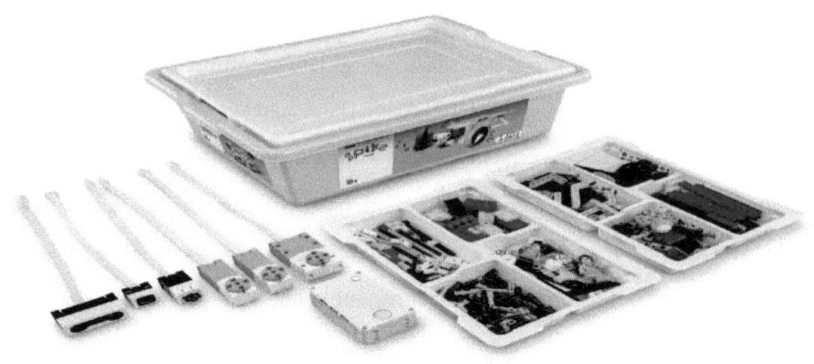

Source: LEGO® Education (2024).

The "heart" of the *LEGO® SPIKE™ PRIME kit* is the Smart *Hub*, which is an advanced programmable block that controls motors and sensors, as well as offering wireless connectivity via *Bluetooth*. This allows students to use a *smartphone* or *tablet* with the SPIKE™ app to bring their robotic creations to life. The *LEGO® Education SPIKE™ Prime Kit* is ideal for elementary to high school students, providing a solid foundation in STEM and coding. The *kit* includes:

- Smart, programmable hub with 6 input/output ports;
- 5 Servomotors (2 large and 3 medium);
- Sensors: Distance, Force, Color and Gyroscope (one of each in the basic kit and a second after purchasing the expansion kit);
- Rechargeable battery and USB charger;
- 528 interchangeable and colorful *LEGO® Technic* pieces.

Figure 3 below shows the electronic components of the *LEGO® SPIKE™ Prime kit*, illustrating some of the essential items described above:

Figure3 - Electronic components of the LEGO® SPIKE™ Prime Kit

Source: LEGO® Education (2024).

4.6.1 The programming environment and its possibilities

SPIKE™ Prime is programmed within the *LEGO® Education SPIKE™ App* programming environment. *SPIKE™ Prime*'s graphical programming language is intuitive and very similar to applications that use block programming language such as *Scratch*, consisting of functional blocks that are organized to build the program. The control program is made up of a set of blocks that allow students to think critically and solve complex problems, regardless of their level of learning.

In it, there are predefined blocks for moving the robot forward for a while, for turning left or right, as well as the option to explore text-based coding with *Python*. The *SPIKE™ Prime* programming environment includes main areas such as the Programming Screen and the Programming Palettes, where all the programming blocks are located and categorized for easy access and organization. As can be seen below:

The *LEGO® Education SPIKE™ Prime* lessons are aligned with the NGSS (Next Generation Science Standards), ISTE (International Society for Technology in Education) and CSTA (Computer Science Teachers Association) educational standards, as well as offering extensions that meet the CCSS (Common Core State Standards) standards for literacy and mathematics. The *LEGO® Education SPIKE™ App* programming environment can be accessed directly on the official LEGO® Education website.

4.6.2 Block programming language

The *LEGO® Education SPIKE™ App* , features a high-level programming environment, where events that will occur during program execution are modeled by function blocks, also known as icon blocks. On the SPIKE™ Prime platform, there are blocks that correspond to actions performed by the LEGO motors® , which will be connected to the smart hub. Sensors and motors can receive and use measured values, integrating them into the program logic. In addition to the blocks that trigger events, there are others that perform logical and mathematical operations, expanding the programming and learning possibilities. Figure 4 shows the learning environment for icon blocks .

Figure4 - Learning environment for icon blocks

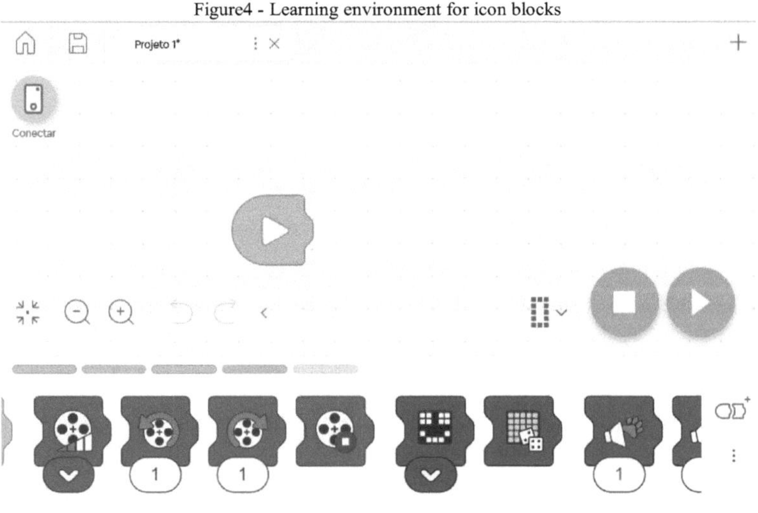

Source: The author (2024)

In this context, and in a similar way to *Scratch*, the *LEGO® Education SPIKE™ App* enables children/adolescents to improve their cognitive skills through programming. As well as sharing their creations, they have access to a variety of existing projects in the platform's virtual environment, which enriches and develops their logical thinking. As Barbosa; Cambruzzi; Cardozo (2015, p. 9) point out:

> "It is in this context of teaching through the concrete and the playful that educational robotics can lead students to explore new ideas, formulate complex reasoning, contextualize and discover new ways of applying concepts acquired in the classroom.

> By using educational robotics to solve problems, students also develop their ability to develop hypotheses, investigate solutions, establish social and group relationships and formulate conclusions."

The *LEGO® Education SPIKE™ App* platform is easy to access and very intuitive, as illustrated by the learning environment for word blocks in (figure 5). This image represents the initial screen of the interface in the word blocks tab, where all the commands are organized for executing the chosen actions and movements.

Figure5 - Learning environment for word blocks

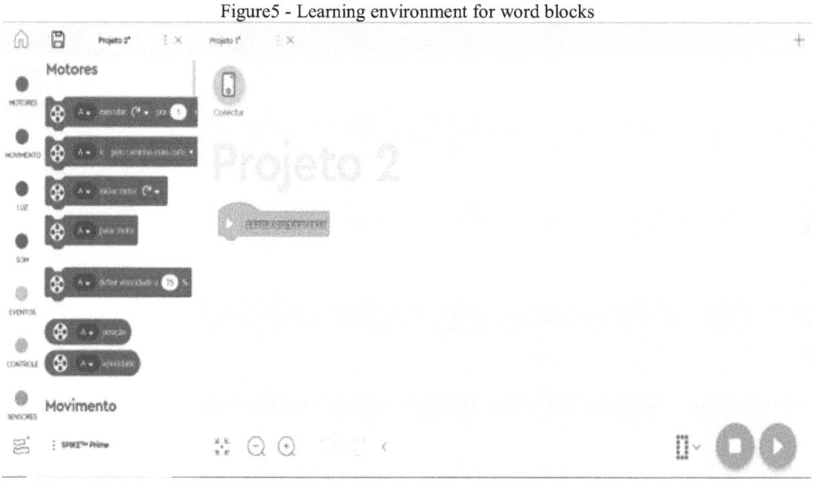

Source: The author (2024)

In (figure 6), you can see on the *LEGO® Education SPIKE™ App* home screen (located on the left) all the operational and relational buttons, organized and differentiated by color and the possibility of adding more blocks. You can also create your own blocks for specific actions. This makes it easier for the user to recognize the function of each button, allowing for a more intuitive execution of the tasks to be performed by the students throughout each activity.

Figure6 - Executable commands

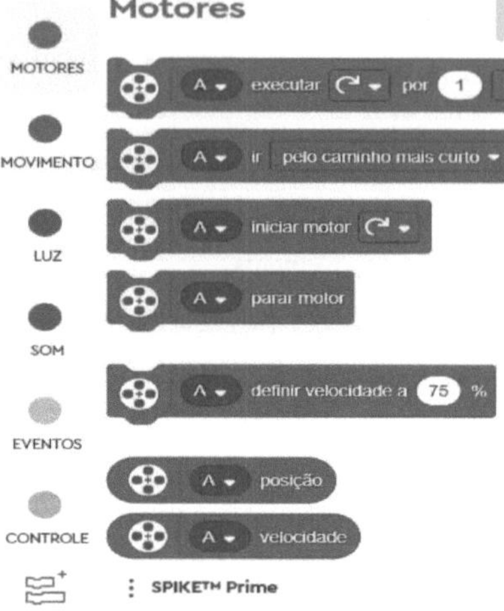

Source: The author (2024)

The platform is full of minute details. It has an intuitive menu so that users can quickly familiarize themselves with its commands, as well as an integrated tutorial menu, which is fed by pre-supplied and pre-molded elements from the platform's library. This facilitates learning and the creation of interactive and educational projects.

4.7 PYTHON PROGRAMMING

It's important to reflect on the role of computational thinking, which is highlighted in the National Common Core Curriculum (BNCC) as a goal for the subject of mathematics in the final stages of primary and secondary education. As described in the BNCC (2018, p. 271),

> [...] learning Algebra, as well as those related to Numbers, Geometry and Probability and Statistics, can contribute to the development of students' computational thinking, given that they need to be able to translate a given situation into other languages, such as transforming problem situations, presented in the mother tongue, into formulas, tables and graphs and vice versa.

Computer programming is becoming increasingly prevalent in society. The job market has a growing demand for professionals with knowledge in this area, even those without technical or higher education training. For this reason, it is believed that programming should be introduced in schools from the earliest grades. The BNCC presents the subject as a facilitator of the learning process.

> [...] the Special Theme digital cultures and computing relates to the approach, at the different stages of Basic Education and by the different curricular components, to the pedagogical use of new communication technologies and the exploitation of these new technologies to understand the world and to act in it. From a critical perspective, information and communication technologies are tools for mediating learning and schools, especially teachers, must help students learn to obtain, transmit, analyze and select information (BNCC, 2018, p. 50).

In relation to children's interaction with technology, it is common to hear comments about the supposed control that computers exert over people. According to Papert (1980/1986, p. 17),

> "From my perspective, it's up to the child to program the computer and, in doing so, they acquire a sense of mastery over one of the most modern and powerful pieces of technological equipment and establish intimate contact with some of the most profound ideas in science, mathematics and the art of constructing intellectual models.

When discussing the concept of programming, Papert (1986, p. 18) describes that "it simply involves dialoguing with the computer in a language that is understandable both to it and to human beings". Using code, the programmer defines commands to be executed, elements to be counted and compared, and the computer carries out the tasks exactly as instructed, following the prescribed sequence. Papert (1986) also points out that it is feasible to learn to interact with computers in a way analogous to learning one's native language, and that this interaction can alter the learning process in other areas. Although technological growth is an important driver in today's market, there is a high drop-out rate in higher education courses related to this area.

In addition, "the process of learning through programming is often marked by trial and error" (CORRÊA, NOTARE, 2019, p. 298). As the authors point out, these errors are seen as conceptual misunderstandings, transforming them from punitive instruments into moments of discovery and understanding, which can significantly enrich teaching and the formation of knowledge.

In the current panorama of computational development, education and the application of digital technologies, the introduction of the teaching of programming logic and the principles of Computer Science from primary school level has been a subject of debate in both academic studies and scientific circles (OLIVEIRA et al., 2014). At the same time, Geraldes (2014) mentions that several campaigns support the integration of programming teaching in conventional schools, without limitations, with the support of prominent figures in the technology sector such as Bill Gates, Mark Zuckerberg and Jack Dorsey, who see school programming as a means of promoting digital inclusion. According to Geraldes (2014), for these influencers, the ability to understand and produce code is as essential as the ability to read and write.

Just as Mathematics fosters the development of Computational Thinking, the latter offers significant contributions to the teaching and understanding of Mathematics. As described in the BNCC (2018, p. 271),

> Associated with computational thinking, it is worth highlighting the importance of algorithms and their flowcharts, which can be studied in math classes. An algorithm is a finite sequence of procedures that enables a given problem to be solved. Thus, the algorithm is the decomposition of a complex procedure into its simplest parts, relating and ordering them, and can be represented graphically by a flowchart. Algorithmic language has points in common with algebraic language, especially in relation to the concept of variable.

According to Barichello (2021, p. 4), "computational thinking is defined as the ability to approach problems using computer science knowledge and techniques, which includes organizing, representing and examining data and processes". In this context, computer programming is used as a tool to organize, represent and examine knowledge in a systematic way.

For the didactic experiment in question, the Python programming language was chosen as the main teaching/learning target. Barichello (2021, p. 4) explains that,

> Programming language: a language used to describe algorithms, written by a human being, which can be understood by a computer. In this case, the term "understand" is being used in the very narrow sense of "follow the steps". Normally, programming languages have a small set of available commands and very strict syntax so that there is no ambiguity when the commands are executed. This can compromise the agility of their use, as it is necessary to know several specific details that may vary from one language to another.

Python is a programming language that can offer functionalities similar to those of a calculator, among others. It has built-in mathematical operators that make it easier to perform calculations and code algebraic expressions. *Python* also has specific functions, such as the // operator, which returns the integer quotient of a division, and the % operator, which gives the remainder of the division, not the percentage, but the value remaining after the division between integers. Figure 7 shows the application of basic operations using the programming language.

Figure7 - Basic mathematical operations with Python

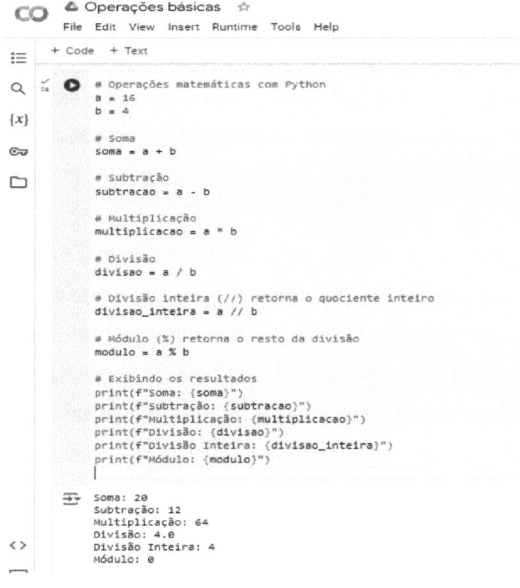

Source: The author (2024)

The ability to adapt and customize codes is one of the aspects that make *Python* a functional and versatile language, in many cases surpassing traditional algebraic methods, which are more rigid and sequential. There are several platforms for programming in *Python*.

IDLE[2] is the standard *Python* integrated development environment, which requires installation and can consume a significant amount of computer memory. To get started using *Python* and simplify access and use for students, we began our work using *Google Collaboratory*, known as *Colab*, which allows you to read and execute Python code (figure 8) directly in the browser, without the need for local installation. Then, after this first contact, we migrated to the *LEGO* platform® *SPIKE™ PRIME App*.

Figure 8 shows the *Google Colab* interface. There is a coding space already filled in where the program asks the user for data to process and return a different result. In the initial line, the variable "a" is used to store the user's answer to the question "Let's find out what year you were born, enter your age:". Since the variables received by the *input* command are interpreted as *strings* (texts), the next line transforms the variable "a" into an integer, renaming it "b". In the third line, the variable c is used to calculate the interval between the current year, 2024, and the user's year of birth, which is inferred by subtracting the user's age (input) from 2024. The fourth line contains the data output instruction, displaying an informative message about the user's year of birth, based on the value obtained from the "c" variable.

The working environment of *LEGO® SPIKE™ PRIME* is an interactive and intuitive platform designed to engage users of all ages in learning fundamental programming and robotics concepts. With a user-friendly interface and visually distinct code blocks, *LEGO® SPIKE™ PRIME* allows users to experiment with building and programming robotic models in a playful and educational way. Interactivity is a strong point, as the platform responds immediately to code instructions, providing visual and physical *feedback* through the robots' movements. This not only makes it easier to understand the effects of the code, but also stimulates problem-solving and creative thinking. Figure 9 shows the *LEGO® SPIKE™ PRIME* programming interface in the *Python* coding environment.

[2] IDLE - (Integrated Development and Learning Environment)

Figure8 - Learning environment for Python

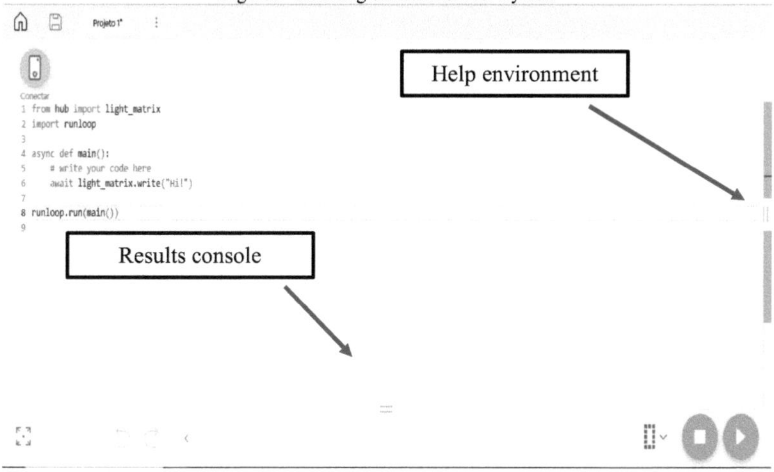

```
from hub import light_matrix
import runloop

async def main():
    # write your code here
    await light_matrix.write("Hi!")

runloop.run(main())
```

Help environment

Results console

Source: The author (2024)

You can see the *LEGO® SPIKE™ PRIME* programming interface. There is a coding space already filled in where the program asks the robot to execute specific movements. The initial line imports the "*MotorPair*" class from the *LEGO® SPIKE™ PRIME* module, which is used to control a pair of motors. Since the movement functions require specific parameters, the next line defines the default speed of the motors and the rotation corresponding to a distance in centimeters. Following the code, the *"wait_for_seconds"* function is used to create a pause in execution, followed by commands that move the motors by a set distance or rotation, exemplifying the data output instruction that activates the robot's movement. In (figure 10) below, we can see the running code of one of the lesson plans, entitled "Training Camp 1", part of PRIME LESSON[3] . This lesson plan is one of many educational resources offered for the use of *LEGO® SPIKE™ PRIME*, designed to promote programming skills and computational thinking.

[3] https://education.lego.com/pt-br/lessons/primecompetition-ready/training-camp-1-driving-around

Figure9 - - Execution of the "Training Camp 1" Python code

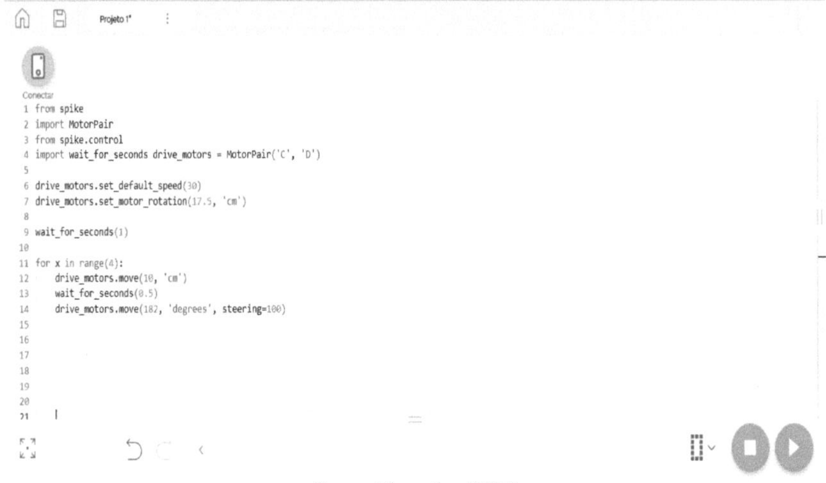

Source: The author (2024)

It is crucial to emphasize the importance of correct syntax in commands. Every parenthesis, quotation mark or sign is essential for the computer to interpret the code properly and perform the operations accurately.

5 METHODOLOGY

5.1 BACKGROUND TO THE STUDY

The research was conducted with 1st year high school students, aged between 14 and 16, with around 20 students separated into 5 groups of 4 students per class time (2 consecutive times of 50 minutes per week), in a school located in Rio de Janeiro, enrolled in the year 2024. The face-to-face meetings took place weekly on Thursday mornings, from March to June 2024, thus configuring the spatial and temporal context of the research.

The school, which caters exclusively for technical secondary education, has 495 students enrolled. Within the context of the research, the institution has a computer lab and a multipurpose room, where the sessions for educational robotics classes were held. In this school, the subject is considered one of the training itineraries, and is taught once a week for two 50-minute classes.

This research is of an applied nature, since its aim is to generate knowledge with practical application. In addition, it has similar characteristics to a case study, since this can be defined as an empirical investigation that examines a contemporary phenomenon in depth and within its real context. Complementing this view, Gil (2019) points out that the case study involves an in-depth and exhaustive examination of one or a few cases, allowing for a broad and detailed knowledge of the research object.

As far as the approach is concerned, this research is qualitative in nature, since the data will not be analyzed using statistical methods. As highlighted by (LÜDKE, 2013) , the qualitative approach is characterized by the use of non-numerical data, presented through verbal descriptions, with the aim of investigating the lived experiences of individuals in complex social contexts. Most research classified as a case study adopts a predominantly qualitative and inclusive approach.

5.2 DATA PRODUCED

With regard to data collection instruments for a case study, this form of research requires the use of various sources of evidence, according to (LÜDKE, 2013, p. 51).

> [...] Based on what he has already obtained, the researcher examines the material again in order to increase his knowledge, discover new angles and deepen his vision. They can also explore the links between the various items, trying to establish relationships and associations and then combining, separating or reorganizing them. Finally, the researcher seeks to broaden the field of information by identifying the emerging elements that need to be explored further.

As (GIL, 2017, p. 63) highlights:

> "Case studies require the use of multiple data collection techniques. The most common are: documentation, interviews and observations. This is important to ensure the necessary depth to the study and the insertion of the case in its context and to give greater credibility to the results."

Borba and Araújo (2020, p. 33) point out that, in the qualitative approach, "formulating a guiding question is a fundamental aspect on which the success of any research depends". The authors also stress that this question is a condensation of the process of choice, stating that "the whole process of constructing the question is part of the question itself" (BORBA; ARAÚJO, 2020, p. 33). For this reason, the first sections of this study outline the motivations for choosing the topic and the concern that generated the guiding questions.

The relevance of the qualitative approach in this study is also justified by the focus on understanding "how" learning takes place. According to Borba and Araújo (2020, p. 24), "the result of the research is intrinsically linked to the objective and methodology employed".

Therefore, in order to obtain results that explore issues such as the role of the teacher in mediating activities with computers, the dynamics of the relationship between teacher and students in virtual environments, or how learning develops with *Python* programming, it is essential that the approach allows for a descriptive and qualitative analysis of teachers' perceptions.

With regard to intensive observations, Marconi and Lakatos (2017, p. 237) explain that this method "uses the senses to capture certain aspects of reality. This is not just about seeing and hearing, but also covers the detailed analysis of facts or phenomena that are the object of study."

5.3 WORKSHOP ORGANIZATION AND PLANNING

This study consists of investigating the responses (table1) and student achievement regarding the impact of Programming with *LEGO® SPIKE™ PRIME* and *Python* on the learning process of robotics and programming concepts among 1st year technical high school students. The research was carried out with students from a school located in Rio de Janeiro during the first semester of 2024. As mentioned above, the activities were carried out in person, in weekly meetings on Thursdays, taking advantage of the facilities available at the school, such as the computer lab and the robotics room.

Table2 - Summary of the survey.

Aspect	Description
Type of Problem Approach	Qualitative research
Nature of the research	Applied
Research objectives	Exploratory, Descriptive
Research participants	Around 100 first-year high school students aged between 14 and 16
Research period	March to June 2024
Search Location	School located in Rio de Janeiro, RJ
Technical Methods Used	Bibliographical Research, Case Study, Practice
Data Collection Instruments	Structured Direct Observation
How the data collection instruments were applied	Structured form

Data Analysis Methods	Qualitative analysis based on observations and notes from the forms

Source: The Author (2024).

The proposed workshop was offered as an extracurricular activity, aimed at classes of the aforementioned target audience, totaling around 20 participants, all aged between 14 and 16. The activity, entitled "Programming with *LEGO® SPIKE™ PRIME App* and *Python*", was designed to teach robotics and programming content using the *LEGO® SPIKE™ PRIME App* platform conjunction with the *Python* language. As there was no need for prior knowledge, the basic concepts of robotics and programming were introduced, exemplified and practiced during the meetings.

The meetings were organized over three months, with the aim of engaging the students in the importance of the topics discussed, teaching the basics of *Python* programming using the *KIT LEGO® SPIKE™ PRIME* , and providing the creation of a final project that integrated all the content covered. In addition, it was essential to carry out an assessment of the students' knowledge before and after the workshop, in order to compare their perceived progress in mastering these topics.

Below, I present the planning for each individual meeting throughout the project. It should be noted that we used the lesson plans from *PRIME LESSONS*. Several adaptations were made, since the plans are only presented in "blocks of words" and in English, and it was necessary to adjust each code for the *Python* language, in all we took the first 10 lessons (table 2) as a basis.

Table3 - Programming lessons in blocks of words for *Python*.

Unit/Lesson
Unit 1
How to use these tutorials?
Building a robot
Easier assembly with Spike Prime
Installing the software & firmware
Unit 2
Getting to know the software
Managing projects
Viewing sensor data

Unit 3
Configuring your robot's movement
Walking in a straight line
Gyroscope curves
More precise curves
Unit 4
Pseudocode
Commenting the code
Unit 5
Introduction to the force sensor
Introduction to the color sensor
Introduction to the distance sensor
Unit 6
Repeating blocks
Using sound blocks & music
Using light blocks
Block if then
Unit 7
Interruption detection
Follow the line
Final challenges
Unit 8
Introduction to events
Event synchronization
Variables
My blocks
Unit 9
Aligning with the line
Proportional line follower
Going straight with the gyroscope
PID line tracker
Unit 10

Debugging techniques
Reliability techniques

Source: The Author (2024).

The classes taught, as detailed in (table 2), were designed to introduce first-year technical high school students to the world of programming. Initially, the students were introduced to block programming. This phase was crucial for building a solid foundation and preparing students for the gradual transition to the *Python* programming language. As they progressed, the students began to explore programming in *Python*, which, being a textual language, offers greater flexibility and power for creating complex solutions. This carefully planned and guided transition allowed students to develop a deeper understanding of programming logic and problem-solving techniques, enabling them to apply this knowledge to practical challenges and projects.

5.4 DATA ANALYSIS

During the case study phase, the data recorded on the forms used to document the direct observations was compiled, as well as the information collected in the intensive observations carried out during the robotics classes. The research involved four programming teams (RobMuts, PinkBots, Mamutes, RobotMar) , identified by names chosen by the students themselves. The results achieved in the missions proposed during the robotics classes, as well as the overall scores for each team, are detailed in Table 4, entitled "Overall Results".

It is important to note that, due to the established scoring rules, there are only three scoring possibilities: 10, 5 and 0. According to the rules, there will never be more than two 10s or more than two 5s, since the maximum score is awarded to the half of the teams that successfully complete the mission first, within the time limit set for the lessons.

In addition, questions were put directly to the students via a questionnaire, with the aim of recording and analyzing their perceptions of the classes. The application of these questionnaires made it possible to quantify the results, as illustrated in units 5, 6, 7 and 8 of (table 3). Considering the answers obtained from 20 students participating in the survey, the data was organized and analyzed according to (table 3), all provided individually on *GoogleForms*.

Table4 - Questionnaires applied in each class.

Possible questions	Answer options	Number of votes			
		10	5	0	Total
Unit 1: have you learned about the LEGO® SPIKE™ PRIME kit?					
Assembling the robot	10 ( ) 5 ( ) 0 ( )				
Install software & firmware	10 ( ) 5 ( ) 0 ( )				
Get to know the LEGO® SPIKE™ PRIME kit	10 ( ) 5 ( ) 0 ( )				
Browse the tutorials	10 ( ) 5 ( ) 0 ( )				
Unit 2: What have you learned about the software?					
Using the software	10 ( ) 5 ( ) 0 ( )				
Managing projects	10 ( ) 5 ( ) 0 ( )				
View sensor data	10 ( ) 5 ( ) 0 ( )				
Unit 3: What have you learned about moving the robot?					
Configuring movement	10 ( ) 5 ( ) 0 ( )				
Walking in a straight line	10 ( ) 5 ( ) 0 ( )				
Making turns with a gyroscope	10 ( ) 5 ( ) 0 ( )				
More precise cornering	10 ( ) 5 ( ) 0 ( )				
Unit 4: What have you learned about Pseudocode and Comments?					
Writing pseudocode	10 ( ) 5 ( ) 0 ( )				
Comment the code	10 ( ) 5 ( ) 0 ( )				
Unit 5: What have you learned about sensors?					
Using the force sensor	10 ( ) 5 ( ) 0 ( )				
Using the color sensor	10 ( ) 5 ( ) 0 ( )				
Using the distance sensor	10 ( ) 5 ( ) 0 ( )				
Unit 6: What have you learned about Repeat Blocks and Conditionals?					
Use repeating blocks	10 ( ) 5 ( ) 0 ( )				
Use sound & music blocks	10 ( ) 5 ( ) 0 ( )				
Use light blocks	10 ( ) 5 ( ) 0 ( )				
If then" block	10 ( ) 5 ( ) 0 ( )				
Unit 7: What have you learned about Programming Challenges?					
Detecting interruptions	10 ( ) 5 ( ) 0 ( )				
Follow the line	10 ( ) 5 ( ) 0 ( )				

Complete the final challenges	10 ( ) 5 ( ) 0 ( )				
Unit 8: What have you learned about the Events and Variables commands?					
Scheduling events	10 ( ) 5 ( ) 0 ( )				
Synchronizing events	10 ( ) 5 ( ) 0 ( )				
Creating and using variables	10 ( ) 5 ( ) 0 ( )				
Use "my blocks"	10 ( ) 5 ( ) 0 ( )				
Unit 9: What have you learned about Advanced Programming Techniques?					
Align with the line	10 ( ) 5 ( ) 0 ( )				
Follow a proportional line	10 ( ) 5 ( ) 0 ( )				
Walking straight with a gyroscope	10 ( ) 5 ( ) 0 ( )				
Follow line with PID	10 ( ) 5 ( ) 0 ( )				
Unit 10: What have you learned about debugging and reliability?					
Acceleration	10 ( ) 5 ( ) 0 ( )				
Debugging techniques	10 ( ) 5 ( ) 0 ( )				
Reliability techniques	10 ( ) 5 ( ) 0 ( )				

Source: The Author (2024).

5.5 DESCRIPTION OF THE DIDACTIC SEQUENCE

The activities developed in the context of Programming classes with word blocks and *Python* were structured as missions, where each successful task resulted in a score recorded on a scorecard, thus applying gamification techniques to the learning environment. This concept involves quantification and numerical recording, which are essential for monitoring student performance.

In our sequence of activities and lessons, each mission represented a specific piece of programming and robotics knowledge that had to be assimilated by the students, and they were sequenced and identified as Mission 1, Mission 2, Mission 3, and so on.

In Unit 1, students were introduced to initial concepts such as "Building a robot" and "Installing the software & firmware". These first missions were key to ensuring that all students were familiar with the basic elements of the *LEGO® SPIKE™ PRIME App*. The students were organized into groups of 4 to 5 people and, after a brief presentation of the topic, began assembling the base robot. During this activity, the teacher circulated around the room, offering support and ensuring that all the groups were prepared for the subsequent challenges.

In the second unit, the focus was on "Getting to know the *software*", "Managing projects", and "Visualizing sensor data". The students, organized in the same groups, explored the programming environment of the *LEGO® SPIKE™ PRIME App*. The teacher demonstrated how to use the app's features and guided the students in practicing these operations. This stage was essential to enable the students to collect and analyze data, fundamental concepts in statistics and applied mathematics.

In the third lesson, the activities focused on "Configuring the movement of your robot", including tasks such as "Walking in a straight line" and "Curves with a gyroscope". The students applied the knowledge they had acquired in the previous lessons to precisely control the movement of their robots. In this activity, they worked with angular measurements and distance, applying geometry concepts and calculating trajectories. The teacher closely monitored the execution of these tasks, offering feedback and helping to correct any errors. This lesson was crucial for developing the practical skills needed for robotics activities.

In the fourth lesson, the students were introduced to the concepts of "Pseudocode" and "Commenting the code". This stage helped the students to plan their algorithms in a structured way and to document their solutions, a vital step in the transition to more complex programming. The students applied these concepts to documenting their programs, with the teacher providing guidance and highlighting the importance of well-structured and documented code

In the fifth lesson, the missions led the students to explore the sensors in the *LEGO® SPIKE™ PRIME* KIT, such as the "Force sensor", "Color sensor", and "Distance sensor". During this phase, the students learned how to use these sensors so that the robot could interact with the environment. The teacher guided the groups in programming the sensors and integrating the data into the students' project, increasing the complexity and interactivity of the robots they built

In the sixth lesson, the students were introduced to the concepts of loops and conditionals, using "Repeat blocks", "Sound & music blocks", "Light blocks", and the "If then block". During this lesson, the students created more dynamic and responsible programs, applying the concepts presented. Here, they worked with conditional logic and Boolean operations, which are essential for creating algorithms. The teacher provided continuous support, helping the students to understand the practical applications of these concepts in creating interactive programs

In the seventh lesson, the students were challenged with practical tasks that consolidated the knowledge they had acquired. The activities included "Interruption Detection" and "Follow the Line", culminating in the "Final Challenges". The groups worked collaboratively to solve the proposed challenges, applying all the knowledge acquired up to that point. In particular, in the "Follow the line" activity, the students applied the concept of proportions by programming a "Proportional line follower", where they dynamically adjusted the robot's parameters based on the sensor readings.

In the eighth lesson, students began working with more abstract concepts that are essential for programming in *Python*, such as events, "event synchronization", and variables. These concepts involve the use of mathematical structures and the manipulation of data which are fundamental to the development of complex algorithms. The students applied these concepts to their projects, with the teacher providing guidance on best practices for dealing with abstractions in programming

In the ninth lesson, advanced *Python* programming techniques were introduced, such as "Aligning with the line" and "Proportional line follower". The students applied these techniques, which involve calculating proportional adjustments and the robots' response based on sensory data. The teacher reviewed the activities carried out, providing detailed *feedback* on the students' performance and highlighting best practices in advanced programming

In the tenth and final class, the focus was on teaching debugging and reliability techniques to improve the robustness of the programs developed. The students learned and applied *debugging* techniques and how to improve the reliability of their programs. The teacher guided the students through the testing and tweaking phase, discussing the importance of debugging in software development and how to ensure that programs work reliably in different situations

This didactic planning allowed the students to progress in a structured way, starting with the fundamentals of assembly and programming with blocks and moving on to complex programming skills in *Python*, using the *LEGO® SPIKE™ PRIME App* as a powerful tool for practical and interactive learning.

5.5.1 SOME MISSIONS

During the meetings, some answers were collected from the groups. It is important to note that no templates were provided for the students. Any algorithmic solution that, when converted into a visual program in blocks in the *LEGO* environment® *SPIKE™ PRIME App*, solved the proposed mission, was considered correct. This approach encouraged the students' creativity and autonomy, allowing for multiple viable solutions to the problems presented, in line with the aim of developing critical thinking and problem-solving skills through programming and robotics. We applied the resolution of the activity proposed in unit 3, in which the teams had to assemble the suggested robots (figure 11) "Droid Bot IV" and "BMA", observing their specificities.

Figure10 - Robot assembly and connectivity

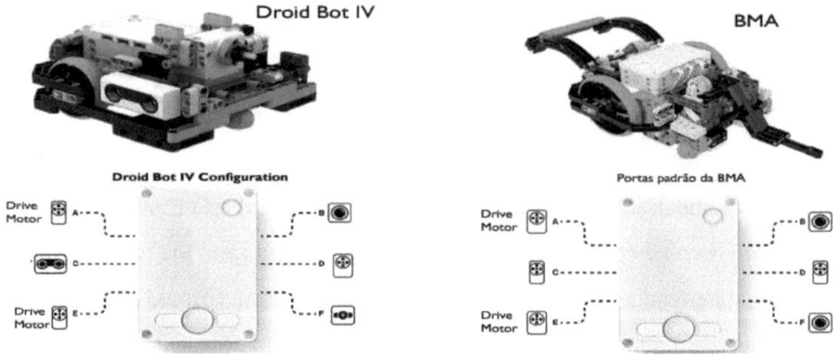

Source: Unit 3 - Prime Lessons (primelessons.org

For the Droid Bot IV, smaller wheels were used, where one revolution corresponds to 17.5 cm. This means that the default movement speed was set to a higher value, due to the shorter distance covered by each rotation.

For the BMA, larger wheels were used, where one revolution corresponds to 27.6 cm. This means that the standard movement speed was set to a lower value, offering greater control due to the longer distance covered by each rotation.

Below (figure 12), we present the codes in word blocks used to configure the movement of the robots. These codes show how to adjust the speed of movement based on the size of the wheels and the rotations of the motors.

Figure11 - Code in word blocks.

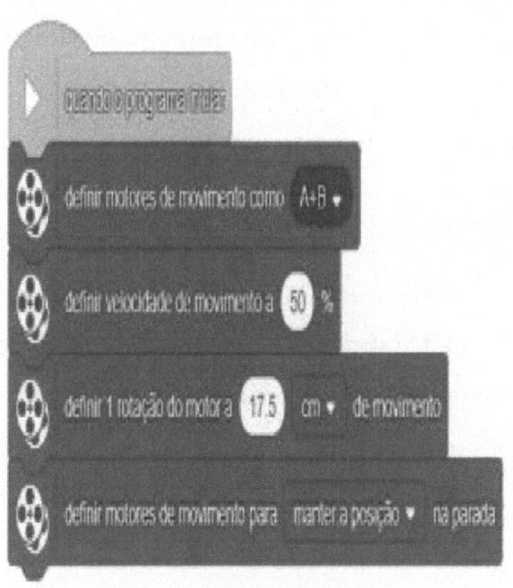

Droid Bot IV

quando o programa iniciar
definir motores de movimento como A+B
definir velocidade de movimento a 25 %
definir 1 rotação do motor a 27.6 cm de movimento
definir motores de movimento para manter a posição na parada

BMA

Source: The author (2024)

Figure 13 shows the Python version of the code, which reflects the same movement logic as previously configured with blocks of words. This code illustrates how students can move from visual to textual programming, while maintaining the principles of controlling the speed and movement of the robots.

Figure12 - Python code

```
# Definindo os motores de movimento
motor_pair = MotorPair('A', 'B')
# Configurando a velocidade de movimento para 50%
motor_pair.set_default_speed(50)
# Movendo o robô para frente por 17.5 cm
motor_pair.move(17.5, 'cm')
# Mantendo a posição após a parada
motor_pair.stop()
```

Droid Bot IV

```
# Definindo os motores de movimento
motor_pair = MotorPair('A', 'B')
# Configurando a velocidade de movimento para 25%
motor_pair.set_default_speed(25)
# Movendo o robô para frente por 27.6 cm
motor_pair.move(27.6, 'cm')
# Mantendo a posição após a parada
motor_pair.stop()
```

BMA

Source: The author (2024)

In the programming environment, students were able to program using Word Blocks or Python, each offering specific benefits. Programming in Word Blocks is visual and intuitive, ideal for beginners. It allowed students to build programs by dragging and connecting blocks, which makes it easier to understand basic concepts such as *loops* and conditionals without having to write code.

Python programming, on the other hand, is textual and offers greater control and flexibility. It is suitable for students who are ready to tackle writing code and exploring more advanced features. Python helps develop deeper coding skills and prepares students for more complex challenges.

6 ANALYSIS OF RESULTS

As a conclusion to the research work, the following results were obtained: Missions 5, 7 and 9 stood out as the most complex challenges, being the only ones not solved by all the teams. In the other challenges, all the teams managed to complete the missions, resulting in the final score shown Table 4. These results suggest that, although most of the missions were accessible to the students, some required a more advanced level of understanding and programming skills, indicating areas for future revisions and improvements to the curriculum. However, the main objective, which was contact and knowledge acquisition, was achieved by the students.

Table5 - Results of the questionnaires applied in each class.

Teams	Overall result
RobMuts	90
PinkBots	55
Mammoths	85
RobotMar	70

Source: The author (2024)

When analyzing the results computed from (table 4), it was observed that, when asked if the knowledge acquired could be applied in other activities, the majority of the students showed insecurity, with 8 out of the 10 challenges opting for "I'm not sure." However, when asked about continuing the robotics classes, all the students expressed a clear desire for them to continue, showing great enthusiasm for the content offered.

From direct observations, it was noted that the students had fun trying to solve the problems, especially due to the playful aspect introduced by the lessons. However, that same game element seems to have encouraged a more hurried approach, where students prioritized speed over careful and strategic analysis of the challenges. So, although gamification motivated the students, it also diverted their focus away from solving the challenges correctly, leading them to adopt a more impulsive attitude, with greater use of trial and error.

The answers to the structured questionnaires also indicated that the students enjoyed the fun aspect of the classes and would recommend the robotics classes to other classmates. They all agreed that the classes should continue, which reinforces the value of these activities in engaging students. However, it was clear that, in the participants' perception, the knowledge of programming logic worked on during the robotics classes was not seen as directly applicable to other areas of knowledge. This suggests that the classes need to incorporate elements of interdisciplinarity more explicitly, especially considering the age group of the students, 14 to 16, where the connection between different areas of knowledge is not yet clearly established. This aspect was underestimated in lesson planning, indicating an area for improvement in future educational projects.

7 CONCLUSIONS

The research work, with a theoretical-practical focus and using a case study as a research technique, proved to be highly effective in allowing theoretical concepts to be applied in practice, within a specific context. The results indicate that practical classes involve students in a process of immersion and experience of theories. In the case of educational robotics, it was evident how the students learn with each other, at their own pace and motivated by the interest aroused by the novelty, which in this context is the introduction to programming logic.

In an attempt to outdo their peers, students tend to abandon the process of analysis and planning and try to solve problems in a hurry and by trial and error. This does not guarantee that the students really understand the solution, but rather that one of their "kicks" ends up being correct. This tendency was confirmed when we asked the students to rewrite their answers without the pressure of competition, by realigning the program blocks or transcribing the algorithm on paper. Few were able to express their answers clearly again.

The use of a visual language, such as programming blocks, to teach programming logic has proved to be extremely efficient, as it focuses the process of creating algorithms on fundamental concepts, without worrying about textual syntax, allowing for greater emphasis on correct logical reasoning.

It is recommended that gamification is not used in every lesson. It is important to wait until the essential concepts have been well assimilated by the students before introducing competition into the activities. However, keeping gamification as a teaching strategy is valuable, because even in an already motivating learning environment, such as that provided by educational robotics, lessons add joy and fluidity to teamwork, promoting natural collaboration between students.

The results obtained from the application of the structured questionnaire in table 3 show that students do not clearly perceive that they are using other knowledge or skills in addition to those taught in programming classes with educational robotics. It is therefore necessary to contextualize the content focused on robot operation and controls with topics from other subjects, such as science and mathematics, to encourage a clear interdisciplinary connection. Reviewing or introducing related topics can be an effective approach; for example, when programming using comparisons, it would be appropriate to review concepts such as ratio and proportion, plane geometry (calculation of area of circle and length). As well as other aspects.

It was concluded that the educational robotics classes contributed to the teaching of programming logic, using a visual programming language in blocks, are highly efficient and exciting. They contribute significantly to the development of sequential logical reasoning, promote teamwork and provide practical experience of the content covered in the classroom. This results in meaningful learning for students, as they put skills and knowledge into practice when solving problems, while the playful aspect generates engagement and favours socialization among students.

8 REFERENCES

ARIMOTO, M. M.; OLIVEIRA, T. D. O. Difficulties in the computer programming learning process: a survey with students from computer science courses. In: XXVII Workshop on Computing Education, 2019, Belém. Proceedings [...]. Belém: [s.n.], 2019. p. 244-254.

BACICH, Lilian; MORAN, José. Active methodologies for innovative education: a theoretical-practical approach. Penso Editora, 2018.

BENNEDSEN, J.; CASPERSEN, M. E. Failure rates in introductory programming: 12 years later. ACM Inroads, New York, v. 10, n. 2, p. 30-36, 2019.

BORBA, Marcelo Carvalho; ALMEIDA, Helber Rangel Formiga Leite de; GRACIAS, Telma. Teaching and classroom research: different voices in an investigation. Belo Horizonte: Autêntica, 2018.

BORBA, Marcelo de Carvalho; ALMEIDA, Helber Rangel Formiga Leite de; GRACIAS, Telma Aparecida de Souza. Research in teaching and the classroom: different voices in an investigation. 2. ed. Belo Horizonte: Autêntica Editora, 2019. (Trends in Mathematics Education Collection).

BOSSE, Y.; GEROSA, M. A. SHARE ON Why is programming so difficult to learn?: Patterns of Difficulties Related to Programming Learning Mid-Stage. ACM SIGSOFT Software Engineering Notes, New York, v. 41, n. 6, p. 1-6, 2016.

BRACKMANN, Christian Puhlmann. Developing computational thinking through unplugged activities in basic education. 2017. 226 f. Thesis (PhD) - Postgraduate Program in Informatics in Education, Center for Interdisciplinary Studies in New Technologies in Education, UFRGS, Porto Alegre, 2017.

BRAZIL. Ministry of Education and Culture. LDB - Law No. 9394/96, December 20, 1996. Establishes the guidelines and bases of National Education. Brasília: [s.n.], 1996.

BRAZIL. Secretariat of Secondary and Technological Education. National Curriculum Parameters: Secondary Education. Part III - Natural Sciences, Mathematics and their Technologies. Brasília: MEC/SEMT, 2000.

BUNDY, Alan. Computational Thinking Is Pervasive. Journal of Scientific and Practical Computing Noted Reviews, v. 1, n. 2, p. 67-69, 2007. Available at: http://www.inf.ed.ac.uk/research/programmes/comp-think/.

CAMBRUZZI, Eduardo; SOUZA, Rosemberg. Educational Robotics in learning Programming Logic: Application and analysis. Anais do Workshop de Informática na Escola, Porto Alegre, v. 21, n. 1, p. 21-28, 2015. DOI: 10.5753/cbie.wie.2015.21.

CAMPOS, Flavio Rodrigues. Educational Robotics in Brazil: Open Issues, Challenges and Future Perspectives. RIEEE - Revista Ibero-Americana de Estudos em Educação, Araraquara, v. 12, n. 4, p. 2108-2121, oct./dec. 2017. DOI: 10.21723/riaee.v12.n4.out./dez.2017.8778.

CARNEIRO, H. G. S.; JUNIOR, A. J. S. Knowledge of Robotics and Mathematics in the initial training of teachers in the Supervised Internship. Educação Matemática Debate, Montes Claros, v. 7, n. 13, p. 1-20, 2023. DOI: 10.46551/emd.v7n13a20.

CASTRO, Adriane de. The use of scratch programming for the development of skills in elementary school children. Revista Tecnologias na Educação, Ponta Grossa, v. 9, n. 19, 2017. Available at: http://tecedu.pro.br/ano9-numerovol19/. Accessed on: May 18, 2024.

CHAVES, Carolina Dias. The use of robotics and programming language activities for the development of computational thinking. Presidente Prudente, 2023. Available at: https://repositorio.unesp.br/server/api/core/bitstreams/874851b7-f6a9-41d3-b49e-1d577651c927/content. Accessed on: [date].

GIL, Antonio Carlos. Methods and techniques of social research. 7. ed. São Paulo: Atlas, 2019.

LEGO. The Lego, Mindstorms EV3. Available at: https://www.lego.com/en-us/mindstorms. Accessed on: May 5, 2024.

LEGO. The Lego, Spike Prime. Available at: https://spike.legoeducation.com/prime/project. Accessed on: May 15, 2024.

LIMA, C. C. de; PREUSS, J. O. Ferramentas Online na Aprendizagem de Programação de Computadores no Contexto do Ensino Remoto. Revista Brasileira de Informática na Educação, v. 31, p. 790-813, 2023. DOI: 10.5753/rbie.2023.2867. Available at: https://journals-sol.sbc.org.br/index.php/rbie/article/view/2867. Accessed on: July 30, 2024.

LIMA, F. R. M. LEGO® ZOOM: a tool for obtaining experimental data in physics for elementary schools. 2017.

LIMA, J. R. T.; FERREIRA, H. S. A Review of National Scientific Productions on the Use of Robotics in Physics Teaching. In: X Encontro Nacional de Pesquisa em Educação em Ciências, Águas de Lindóia-SP, 2015, p. 1-8.

LÜDKE, M.; ANDRÉ, M. E. D. A. Pesquisa em educação: Abordagens qualitativas. São Paulo: EPU, 1986.

LÜDKE, M.; ANDRÉ, M. E. D. A. A pesquisa em educação: abordagens qualitativas. 2. ed. Rio de Janeiro: E.P.U., 2013.

LUZ, A. M. R.; ALVARES, B. A. Physics context & applications. São Paulo: Scipione, 2013.

MALHEIROS, Ana Paula dos Santos. Online mathematics education: the development of modeling projects. 2008.

MAIA, L. D. O. et al. Robotics as a Programming Environment Using the Lego Mindstorms Kit. In: Brazilian Symposium on Informatics in Education, 2008, Brazil.

MARQUES, D.; COSTA, L.; SILVA, M.; REBOUÇAS, A. Attracting High School Students to Computing: A Practical Experience of Introduction to Programming using Games and Python. In: Workshop de Informática na Escola, 2011. Available at: http://milanesa.ime.usp.br/rbie/index.php/wie/article/view/1954.

MORAES, M. C. Learning environments as an expression of coexistence and transformation. In: MORAES, M. C.; BATALLOSO NAVAS, J. M. (Orgs). Complexity and transdisciplinarity in education: theory and teaching practice. Rio de Janeiro: Wak Editora, 2010.

NUNES, Thalia et al. Pedagogical Robotics as a Tool for Learning in Early Childhood Education and Elementary School: A Study in Bibliographic References. In: Congresso Nacional de Educação Infantil e Ensino Fundamental I, Alta Cruz, 2020, p. 221-232.

PERIN, Andréa Pavan; CAMPOS, Celso Ribeiro. Interfaces between Mathematical Modeling, Reasoning and Statistical Thinking. Educação Matemática Debate, Montes Claros, v. 4, n. 10, p. 1-22, 2020. DOI: 10.46551/emd.e202032. Available at: https://www.periodicos.unimontes.br/index.php/emd/article/view/2724. Accessed on: June 30, 2024.

SIQUEIRA, Pedro Vinicius Ramos. Come back, Lin!: Toy maker. -- UFRJ, 2021. 213 f.

SILVA, Maria Aparecida de Faria da; OLIVEIRA, Márcia. Educational Robotics from the Perspective of Active Methodologies. In: WORKSHOP DE INFORMÁTICA NA ESCOLA (WIE), 25., 2019, Brasília. Proceedings [...]. Porto Alegre: Brazilian Computer Society, 2019, p. 1289-1293. DOI: 10.5753/cbie.wie.2019.1289.

SILVA NETO, V. J. da; BONACELLI, M. B. M.; PACHECO, C. A. The Digital Technological System: artificial intelligence, cloud computing and Big Data. Revista Brasileira de Inovação, v. 19, p. e0200024, 2020. DOI: 10.20396/rbi.v19i0.8658756.

VIEIRA, K. D.; HAI, A. A. Computational thinking in education for a curriculum integrated with culture and the digital world. Acta Scientiarum. Education, v. 45, n. 1, p. e52908, 6 oct. 2022.

WING, Jeannette M. Computational thinking. Communications of the ACM, v. 49, n. 3, p. 33, 2006. ISSN 00010782. Available at

WING, Jeannette M. Computational thinking and thinking about computing. Philosophical Transactions of the Royal Society A: Mathematical, Physical and Engineering Sciences, v. 366, n. 1881, p. 3717-3725, 2008. ISSN 1364503X.

YIN, Robert K. Case study: planning and methods. 5. ed. Porto Alegre: Bookman, 2015.

Printed by Books on Demand GmbH, Norderstedt / Germany